ADULT READING SERIES

Challenger

Answer Key

FOR BOOKS 1 - 4

ISBN 0-88336-789-0

© 1985, 1991
New Readers Press
Publishing Division of Laubach Literacy International
Box 131, Syracuse, New York 13210

EACH ONE TEACH ONE

Printed in the United States of America

Cover by Chris Steenwerth

9 8 7 6 5 4 3 2

Book 1

Lesson 1

1 Copying Sentences
See student text.

2 Word Sounds
1. Tim, time
2. tube, tub
3. not, note
4. can, cane
5. quit, quite

Lesson 2

1 Copying Sentences
See student text.

2 Word Sounds
1. huge
2. cut
3. met
4. us
5. cope
6. rode
7. hopes
8. at

Lesson 3

1 Word Sounds
1. mad, mud, made
2. hot, hates, hat
3. six, sit, sip
4. cop, cope, cup
5. man, men, mine
6. us, fuse, used
7. at, as, am
8. late, dates, Kate
9. pet, pep, pen

2 Marking the Vowels
1. fīr¢
2. sĭp
3. cān¢
4. nīc¢
5. wŏk¢
6. sŭn
7. hōl¢
8. bĕd
9. āt¢
10. ūs¢
11. mē
12. lĭd
13. jăb
14. cūt¢
15. kēēp
16. rūl¢

Lesson 4

1 Word Sounds
1. cute
2. tub
3. rod
4. Cape
5. ripe
6. rid
7. wine
8. fad
9. hope
10. fuss
11. let
12. feel
13. hot
14. ham
15. feed

2 Yes or No
Answers will vary.

Lesson 5

1 Adding -ed
1. looked
2. lasted
3. talked
4. asked
5. messed
6. relaxed
1. faced
2. saved
3. joked
4. hired
5. lined
6. refused
1. hopped
2. sipped
3. patted
4. gunned
5. popped
6. sobbed

2 Word Sounds
1. phone
2. bus
3. sale
4. bed
5. pan
6. red
7. cane
8. hut
9. bone
10. hugs
11. horn
12. name
13. park
14. lap

Lesson 6

1 Adding -ed
1. called
2. hunted
3. landed
4. walked
5. dumped
6. mended
1. baked
2. named
3. liked
4. dated
5. tired
6. hoped
1. robbed
2. kidded
3. ripped
4. netted
5. topped
6. rammed

2 Word Sounds
1. sick
2. sent
3. hunt
4. damp
5. ducked
6. hand
7. kick
8. pond
9. sent
10. neck
11. end

Lesson 7

1 Adding -ing
1. going
2. fixing
3. singing
4. looking
5. missing
1. taking
2. having
3. baking
4. joking
5. hoping
1. running
2. sipping
3. patting
4. jabbing
5. hopping

Lesson 8

1 Word Sounds
1. code
2. fox
3. dam
4. pad
5. dive
6. tame
7. rate
8. dined

2 Using a and an
1. an
2. a
3. a
4. an
5. an
6. a
7. a
8. a
9. an
10. an

3 Marking the Vowels
1. fūm¢
2. lĕss
3. nĕck
4. rōb¢
5. tĭck
6. hănd
7. sŏck
8. sāf¢
9. quĭck
10. cĕnt
11. mīnd
12. rēfūs¢
13. ŭs
14. bēēf
15. fēmāl¢

4 Words That Mean the Same
1. huge
2. keep
3. seek
4. honk
5. six
6. jab
7. fix
8. fun
9. weep
10. females

5 Writing Sentences
Answers will vary.

Lesson 9

1 Adding -y to Words
1. messy
2. fussy
3. bumpy
4. needy
5. robbery
1. icy
2. nosy
3. lacy
4. bony
5. wiry
1. funny
2. sunny
3. Mommy
4. Daddy
5. nutty

2 **Words That End in -ly**
1. quickly   4. friendly
2. lovely   5. weekly
3. safely

3 **Words That End in -y**
1. baby   6. Andy
2. candy   7. muddy
3. sixty   8. handy
4. lobby   9. forty
5. ninety   10. Bucky

4 **Words That Mean the Same**
1. hide   7. joke
2. behind   8. refuse
3. ten cents 9. funny
4. male   10. jack
5. not happy 11. Sunday
6. mock   12. Saturday

Lesson 10

1 **Word Sounds**
1. gas, pass
2. fact, acts
3. None, one, done
4. knew, few, new
5. right, lights, night
6. see, fee, knee
7. wrote, note, vote
8. heck, neck, wreck
9. dock, locked, knock
10. lay, way, day

2 **Word Opposites**
1. night   6. huge
2. last   7. wrong
3. back   8. play
4. bad   9. there
5. sad   10. same

3 **Word Study**
1. yesterday   6. females
2. friend   7. wine
3. foot   8. numb
4. ant   9. cot
5. sun   10. fit

Lesson 11

1 **Adding -er to Words**
1. quicker | 1. finer | 1. bigger
2. tighter | 2. ruder | 2. fatter
3. fewer | 3. cuter | 3. hotter
4. boxer | 4. baker | 4. winter
5. hunter | 5. later | 5. hitter
6. burner | 6. diner | 6. mugger

2 **Words that End in -er**
1. bumper   5. pepper
2. hammer   6. ruler
3. Copper   7. worker
4. summer   8. better, better

3 **Changing y to i and Adding -er**
handier   1. luckier
happier   2. happier
luckier   3. lovelier
lovelier   4. fussier
fussier   5. bumpier
bumpier   6. handier

4 **Who Does What?**
1. a hunter   5. a banker
2. a writer   6. a fighter
3. a singer   7. a player
4. a joker   8. a thinker

Lesson 12

1 **Context Clues**

five, work, house

eat, meat, boiled, tea, mug, fork

soap, water, night (water, soap, night)

2 **Word Sounds**
1. deer   8. peas   15. mouse
2. road   9. soak   16. coals
3. due   10. moon   17. main
4. far   11. pain   18. dirt
5. barn   12. foot   19. bored
6. ails   13. maid   20. hard
7. load   14. real

3 **Writing Sentences**
Answers will vary.

Lesson 13

1 **Word Sounds**
1. moon   11. meal   21. lean
2. noon   12. mean   22. lead
3. soon   13. code   23. leaf
4. mail   14. cope   24. worn
5. main   15. cone   25. horn
6. maid   16. tore   26. corn
7. carve   17. sore   27. torn
8. cart   18. wore   28. born
9. card   19. more
10. meat   20. leak

2 **Words That End in -er**
1. painter   4. boarder   7. helper
2. keeper   5. voter   8. teacher
3. catcher   6. diner

3 **Word Study**
1. head   6. air
2. year   7. food
3. pear   8. tea
4. dice   9. fake
5. oven   10. wages

4 **Marking the Vowels**
1. ădd   9. fūmȩ
2. bītȩ   10. rēēl
3. gātȩ   11. hīkȩ
4. dămp   12. hŭnt
5. sĕnd   13. dōzȩ
6. clŏck   14. dŭnk
7. pŏp   15. zōnȩ
8. sāmȩ   16. dĕck

Lesson 14

1 **The Ending -ful**
handful   1. useful
harmful   2. handful
helpful   3. helpful
careful   4. harmful
useful   5. careful
thankful   6. thankful

2 **The Ending -less**
harmless   1. jobless
helpless   2. careless
hopeless   3. homeless
homeless   4. harmless
careless   5. hopeless
jobless   6. helpless

3 **Words That Mean the Same**
1. carve   6. shout
2. ill   7. hurt
3. handy   8. bare
4. film   9. poor
5. soaked   10. dead

4 **Word Opposites**
1. cold   6. messy
2. start   7. others
3. day   8. false
4. worse   9. dumb
5. take   10. harmless

5 **Sayings**
1. told   6. hills
2. call   7. ball
3. cold   8. will
4. bell   9. fall
5. milk   10. fill

Lesson 15

1 The Ending -est
1. nearest
2. cheapest
3. richest
4. smartest
5. loudest

1. finest
2. safest
3. rudest
4. ripest
5. latest

1. biggest
2. hottest
3. fattest
4. maddest
5. reddest

2 Changing y to i and Adding -est
funniest
happiest
luckiest
fussiest
loveliest

1. loveliest
2. fussiest
3. luckiest
4. happiest
5. funniest

3 Word Sounds
1. chess
2. odd
3. sharp
4. talked
5. wall
6. loaf
7. case
8. vote
9. Last
10. well

4 Words That Mean the Same
1. wish
2. drop
3. torn
4. tug
5. queer
6. faint
7. chair
8. boring
9. two
10. must

Lesson 16

1 Word Sounds
1. mouse, house
2. blouse
3. coast
4. toast
5. roast
6. flew
7. new
8. blew
9. pale
10. stale
11. tales
12. slip
13. dip
14. ship
15. each
16. reach
17. bleached, beach
18. rage
19. stage
20. page
21. plain, pain
22. stains
23. shame, lame
24. blamed, same
25. rush, slush
26. blush
27. platter, shattered
28. matter
29. map
30. clapped
31. nap, slap

2 Compound Words
1. downtown
2. baseball
3. football
4. cupcakes
5. cookbook
6. lifeboat
7. weekend
8. homework
9. household
10. sunshine

3 Writing Sentences
Answers will vary.

Lesson 17

1 Word Sounds
1. blow
2. flow
3. slow, row
4. price
5. pride, prizes
6. toast
7. taste, tested
8. best
9. chest, vests
10. pests
11. clown, gown, brown
12. trunk
13. truck
14. trust
15. harming
16. farm, charming
17. clay, may
18. prayed, hay
19. drops, stopped
20. crops
21. gum, plums
22. drum

2 Putting Words into Classes

Town	School	Farm
bus stops	classes	barn
churches	courses	cows
parks	homework	crops
stores	reading	hay
street lights	teachers	hens

3 Best and Least
Answers will vary.

Lesson 18

1 Word Sounds
1. lift
2. left
3. gift
4. shift
5. math, bath
6. path
7. hill
8. spilled
9. grilled
10. chill
11. dare
12. fare
13. spare
14. flares
15. spit
16. pit
17. lit
18. fibs
19. bib, crib
20. ribs
21. coach
22. coast
23. coals

2 Numbers
1. eighteen
2. twenty
3. fifteen
4. fifteen
5. sixteen
6. eleven
7. fifteen
8. seven
9. four
10. thirteen
11. seven
12. twelve
13. Answers may vary.
14. four (or five counting the spare)
15. Answers will vary.
16. Answers will vary.
17. Answers will vary.
18. Answers will vary.
19. Answers will vary.
20. nine

3 Compound Words
1. armchair
2. sunburn
3. bathroom
4. notebook
5. popcorn
6. bedroom
7. checkbook
8. shortstop
9. pancakes
10. downstairs

Lesson 19

1 Word Sounds
1. list	4. math	7. spilled	10. threw
2. flops	5. egg	8. fork	11. cream
3. boss	6. other	9. wipe	12. snow

2 Colors
1. white	3. red	5. black	7. blue
2. Pink	4. green	6. brown	8. gold

3 Which Word Does Not Fit?
1. drive	4. body	7. shrimp	10. yard
2. bedroom	5. raw	8. Christmas	11. slacks
3. neck	6. whale	9. number	12. dune

4 Words That Begin with *un-*
unsafe	1. unhappy
unless	2. unless
unlucky	3. unlucky
unhappy	4. unsafe
unwrapped	5. unwrapped

5 Words That Begin with *re-*
refuse	1. return
remain	2. repaid
remind	3. refuse
repaid	4. remind
return	5. remain

Lesson 20

1 Word Sounds
1. found, ground	7. carve, starve
2. step	8. but, butter
3. marry	9. sweating, sweater
4. pity, city	10. crawl
5. steep	11. hard, hardly
6. Ms., Miss, Ms., Mrs.	12. stood, wood, hood

2 Putting Words into Classes
Breakfast	Dinner	Snacks
corn flakes	pork chops	candy bar
French toast	rice and beans	Coke
fried eggs	roast beef	ice cream cone
ham and eggs	spare ribs	popcorn
pancakes	stuffed peppers	pretzels

3 Twelve Questions
1. true	7. false
2. false	8. true
3. false	9. true
4. Either true or false	10. false
5. false	11. false
6. false	12. Answers will vary.

4 Writing Sentences
Answers will vary.

First Review

1 Choosing the Right Answer
1. bull	4. tall	7. heart	10. been
2. vase	5. Coast	8. ear	11. care
3. sick	6. close	9. anywhere	12. bless

2 Words That Mean the Same
1. scrub	5. cash	9. gleam
2. swift	6. crazy	10. patch
3. useful	7. strange	
4. mock	8. faint	

3 Word Opposites
1. tired	6. awake
2. fire	7. thick
3. answer	8. calm
4. waste	9. tame
5. huge	10. loaf

4 Using *a* and *an*
1. an	6. an
2. a	7. a
3. an	8. a
4. an	9. a
5. an	10. a

5 Putting Words in Classes
Land	Sky	Water
cities	fog	boats
farms	moon	fish
houses	rain	ships
weeds	snow	waves
woods	stars	whales

Second Review

1 Choosing the Right Answer
1. helpless	5. That's	9. unsafe
2. handful	6. I've	10. guilty
3. sadly	7. Didn't	
4. cellar	8. writer	

2 Numbers
1. twelve	6. seven
2. seven	7. sixteen
3. sixty	8. two
4. Answers will vary.	9. one
5. thirteen	10. millions

3 Which Word Fits Best?
1. father	3. pig	5. worst	7. ceiling
2. slacks	4. hushed	6. upset	8. snail

4 Word Pairs
1. salt and pepper	7. reading and writing
2. bride and groom	8. rod and reel
3. Saturday and Sunday	9. black and blue
4. knife and fork	10. cats and dogs
5. ham and eggs	11. snakes and snails
6. soap and water	12. thick and thin

5 Writing Sentences
Answers will vary.

Book 2

Lesson 1

1 About the Reading

1. People cover their noses when they sneeze so their germs won't go all over the room.
2. When somebody sneezes, people often say, "God bless you."
3. dust, cat hairs, weeds, black pepper, colds (any three)
4. 17 years old
5. 6 months
6. Answers will vary.

2 Word Sounds

1. cape   shape
   grape
   shape
2. drink   think
   stink
   think
3. change   change
   range
   strange
4. chew   grew
   grew
   knew
5. cries   tries
   dries
   tries

6. blob   snob
   job
   snob
7. blown   known
   grown
   known
8. smelling   Smelling
   spelling
   swelling
9. broke   smoke
   choke
   smoke
10. bluffed   stuffed
    puffed
    stuffed

3 Matching

1. hearing
2. seeing
3. touching
4. tasting
5. smelling

4 Marking the e's

1. thēs¢
2. ĕnd
3. alon¢
4. blēēd
5. harmlĕss
6. nĕxt
7. us¢ful
8. pancak¢
9. rēmind
10. swĕat
11. clos¢
12. choos¢

5 Words That Sound the Same

1. I, eye
2. hear, here
3. Two, to
4. Dear, deer
5. four, for
6. knows, nose

Lesson 2

1 About the Reading

1. United States
2. more than 28 million
3. $415,000
4. doctor
5. Cats can see better in dim light.
6. Answers will vary.

2 Word Sounds

1. brand   stand
   grand
   stand
2. creeps   creeps
   jeeps
   sleeps
3. fang   slang
   sang
   slang
4. bean   mean
   clean
   mean
5. clear   hear
   hear
   near

6. shrill   shrill
   skill
   spill
7. brown   crown
   clown
   crown
8. paw   paw
   raw
   straw
9. cow   Now
   how
   now
10. sends   spends
    spends
    tends

3 Putting Words in Classes

List A — Cats	List B — Dogs
always land on their feet	barking
climbing trees	chasing cars
nine lives	digging up bones
purring	man's best friend

4 Words That Sound the Same

1. By, buy
2. knew, new
3. ate, eight
4. Do, due
5. Our, hour

Lesson 3

1 About the Reading

1. seven years
2. Rome
3. dead
4. You will have seven years bad luck.
5. Every cell is renewed.
6. Answers will vary, depending on how heavily one smokes.

2 Word Sounds

1. blink   think
   drink
   think
2. brave   brave
   cave
   wave
3. blame   game
   game
   frame
4. blink   drink
   drink
   stink
5. dice   dice
   price
   spice

6. dated   stated
   plated
   stated
7. bone   throne
   cone
   throne
8. chart   part
   part
   start
9. cheek   week
   peek
   week
10. chins   sins
    grins
    sins

3 Word Sounds

Cow	Slow
clown	blow
crowd	grown
how	know
now	show
wow	snow

4 Number Words

1. twenty-four
2. thirty-one
3. thirty
4. fifty
5. forty
6. twenty-five
7. Answers will vary.
8. Answers will vary.
9. Answers will vary, depending on state law.
10. Answers will vary, depending on state law.

Lesson 4

1 About the Reading

1. pub
2. pint and quart
3. He gave away 30,000 gallons of beer as a gift to the gods.
4. They had run out of beer, which served as food, and they needed to find more food.
5. Beer left in sunlight turns cloudy and takes on a funny smell and taste.
6. People who really like beer say it should be served with a head on it.
7. "Minding your p's and q's" means being careful or watching your step.
8. 1620

2 Word Sounds

1. brewed — brewed
   chewed
   stewed
2. colds — holds
   folds
   holds
3. change — strange
   range
   strange
4. beans — beans
   jeans
   means
5. ate — ate
   date
   state
6. found — pound
   pound
   sound
7. dunes — prunes
   prunes
   tunes
8. cream — cream
   dream
   stream

3 Word Sounds

1. stairs, pair, chairs
2. proud, cloud, loud
3. brave, waves, cave
4. cried, tried, dried
5. hear, clear, near
6. range, change, strange
7. mean, beans, jeans
8. lunch, munched, bunch
9. trick, bricks, stick
10. shape, cape, grape

4 Smallest and Biggest

1. second	hour
2. day	month
3. city	country
4. hundred	million
5. shrimp	human being
6. ounce	quart
7. pint	gallon
8. light bulb	sun
9. bike	ship
10. shrimp	roast beef
11. chestnut	tree
12. Rome	world

5 Word Opposites

1. clear
2. ugly
3. anger
4. children
5. always
6. grew
7. sea
8. saved
9. change
10. brand-new

Lesson 5

1 About the Reading

1. 1875
2. scribe
3. 1,875,000
4. 1,984,000
5. Answers will vary.
6. Answers will vary. Acceptable answers include that people did not have telephones and that visiting people who lived some distance away was more difficult in the 1800's than it is today.

2 Word Sounds

1. telling
2. passed
3. mail
4. life
5. six
6. more
7. vowels
8. such
9. still
10. song

3 Who Does What?

1. cab driver
2. baseball player
3. teacher
4. doctor
5. cowboy
6. tailor
7. clown
8. painter
9. preacher
10. scribe

4 Words That Sound the Same

1. write, right
2. whole, hole
3. beat, beet
4. fare, fair
5. meet, meat
6. heard, herd
7. sale, sails
8. won, one

5 Marking Vowels

1. frām¢
2. brănd
3. ōwn
4. pīnt
5. cāv¢
6. grĭn
7. tĕnd
8. măss
9. trĭck
10. spĕnd
11. spīc¢
12. thrōn¢

Review: Lessons 1-5

1 Choosing the Answer
1. fifty
2. talk
3. sense
4. lace
5. mate
6. meant
7. blob
8. bluffing
9. renew
10. deadly

2 Number Words
1. seven
2. fifty-two
3. sixteen
4. eight
5. two
6. two
7. four
8. thirteen
9. fifty
10. seven
11. 19__-1620 = the answer.
12. One thousand

3 Facts
1. sight
2. hearing
3. taste
4. touch
5. smell

Lesson 6

1 About the Reading
1. wool, animal hair, gold
2. bee's wax
3. He began to lose his hair at an early age.
4. These wigs were huge, covering people's backs and floating down over their chests.
5. 12 years
6. Many years ago in Egypt, the bigger a person's wig was, the more important the person was.
7. Answers will vary.

2 Word Sounds
1. shave
2. bangs
3. hair
4. which
5. Feeling
6. Fighting
7. bugs
8. stand
9. scares
10. takes

3 Which Word Does Not Fit?
1. month
2. English
3. catbird
4. scribe
5. start
6. Anne
7. queen
8. wrist
9. cure
10. pound

4 Vowel Sounds

Long Sound for *ea*	Short Sound for *ea*
1. bean	1. bread
2. beat	2. breakfast
3. easy	3. dead
4. please	4. instead
5. squeak	5. sweat

5 Compound Words
1. bath + room
2. big + wig
3. break + fast
4. cat + bird
5. check + book
6. every + thing
7. ginger + bread
8. girl + friend
9. short + stop
10. sun + burn

Lesson 7

1 About the Reading
1. The liquid comes from two pouches under the skunk's tail.
2. A skunk can spray his liquid from a range of ten to twelve feet.
3. He has to wait one week before he can spray again.
4. A skunk sprays his liquid to ward off danger.
5. He faces whatever he thinks is chasing him.
   He stamps his forefeet.
   He raises all but the tip of his tail.
   He raises the tip of his tail and sprays his liquid.
6. You can bathe in tomato juice.

2 Words That Mean the Same
1. munch
2. hidden
3. creep
4. dim
5. sprint
6. touch
7. bluff
8. friendly
9. trouble
10. form

3 Word Opposites
1. a nobody
2. late
3. hard
4. nothing
5. sink
6. stand
7. find
8. forget
9. saved
10. lovely

4 Compound Words
1. bed + room
2. blood + stream
3. cow + boy
4. home + work
5. May + flower
6. note + book
7. side + ways
8. some + one
9. sun + light
10. what + ever

5 Silly Verses
1. state, straight, sky, cry, dates
2. France, pants, tried, cried, dance
3. sour, hour, life *or* wife, life *or* wife, shower

Lesson 8

1 About the Reading
1. Otherwise the older baby chicks might kill the younger ones.
2. They are timing their hatching.
3. Air must get into the eggshell.
4. Someone in the first book of the Bible thinks the chicken came first.
5. The man who wrote this story thinks the egg came first.
6. In this story, *clutch* means a brood of baby chicks or a group of eggs.
7. *Clutch* can also mean a pedal on a standard shift vehicle, a strong grasp, or to hold tightly.

2 Word Sounds

1. laying   laying
   paying
   saying
2. shell   shell
   smell
   spell
3. pounds   pounds
   rounds
   sounds
4. bite   white
   kite
   white
5. claw   raw
   raw
   thaw
6. fail   fail
   mail
   pail
7. bust   just
   dust
   just
8. bends   spends
   lends
   spends
9. cared   scared
   glared
   scared
10. hatch   hatch
    patch
    scratch

3 Which Word Fits Best?

1. glass
2. sky
3. pack
4. upset
5. England
6. Wednesday
7. armchair
8. foot
9. school
10. lung

4 Compound Words

1. babysit
2. copycat
3. handwriting
4. hideout
5. lifetime
6. necktie
7. nickname
8. rainbow
9. touchdown
10. wristwatch

1. touchdown
2. necktie
3. wristwatch
4. hideout
5. copycat
6. handwriting
7. babysit
8. nickname
9. rainbow
10. lifetime

5 Word Sounds

Book	School
1. foot	1. groom
2. hood	2. pool
3. took	3. shoot
4. wood	4. spoon
5. wool	5. tooth

Lesson 9

1 About the Reading

1. California
2. John Sutter
3. 1849
4. forty-niners
5. one ounce

2 Word Sounds

1. bread   spread
   dead
   spread
2. bought   thought
   fought
   thought
3. blind   find
   find
   mind
4. fool's   fool's
   cool's
   pool's
5. leans   means
   cleans
   means
6. boil   soil
   soil
   spoil
7. beached   preached
   preached
   reached
8. leaks   speaks
   sneaks
   speaks

3 Vowels + the letter l

1. belt
2. tall
3. roll
4. milk
5. gold
6. bulb
6. wall
8. bell
9. cold
10. bald
11. Jill, hill

4 Marking the Vowels

1. līce
2. egghĕad
3. wăx
4. wĭthĭn
5. flōat
6. rēason
7. rāise
8. grāve
9. knēē-dēēp
10. nĕst
11. Frănce
12. brāke
13. betwēēn
14. jŭst
15. hătch
16. tĭp
17. sīnce
18. wēak

5 Matching

1. coffee
2. peach
3. chocolate
4. bigwig
5. yolk
6. March
7. kneel
8. lice
9. news
10. hangover

Lesson 10

1 About the Reading

1. Boston
2. 1760
3. No
4. to carry soup
5. to taste the soup before the queen tried it
6. They ran off to get married.
7. The rhymes had been around for hundreds of years before they were called Mother Goose rhymes.
8. Answers will vary. Children like their rhymes, rhythms, and content.

2 Word Sounds

1.	born corn horn	horn	6.	block clock shock	clock
2.	die pie tie	pie	7.	door poor floor	door
3.	close nose rose	nose	8.	free three tree	three
4.	bed fed red	bed	9.	cane crane lane	lane
5.	feet sheet street	street	10.	drum plum slum	plum

3 Which Word Does Not Fit?

1. California
2. snow
3. spring
4. pound
5. eggs
6. leaves
7. ice
8. straw
9. air
10. wool
11. cowboys
12. smoker
13. beach
14. punt

4 Silent Letters

1. knit
2. breath
3. clutch
4. crane
5. wrong
6. thumb
7. wrist
8. climb
9. meant
10. heart
11. lamb
12. watch

5 Words That Sound the Same

1. red, read
2. see, sea
3. weak, week
4. through, threw
5. bear, bare
6. way, weigh
7. break, brake
8. sense, cents

Review: Lessons 1-10

1 Choosing the Answer

1. soundly
2. though
3. shame
4. peeped
5. burp
6. sin
7. main
8. spoil
9. guess
10. hunch

2 Words That Mean the Same

1. shut
2. glitter
3. tease
4. guide
5. spoil
6. break
7. dirt
8. brake
9. melt
10. slim
11. rhyme
12. during

3 Word Opposites

1. death
2. cloudy
3. rare
4. against
5. thaw
6. evening
7. messy
8. shut
9. forgot
10. crooked
11. weak
12. lies

Lesson 11

1 About the Reading

1. We are trying to draw in more air.
2. a. Body heat goes down.
   b. Brain waves become more even.
3. a. The heart rate slows down.
   b. The body relaxes.
   c. Breathing becomes very even.
4. Most dreaming happens during the deepest stage of sleep called REM.
5. You would take quite a few seconds to move.
6. You would probably become quite sick.
7. Answers will vary. Everyone dreams. Dreams are often related to recent events or needs the dreamer has.
8. Answers will vary.

2 Word Sounds

1. paws, claws
2. thaws, straw
3. jaw, law
4. dawn, lawn
5. pawns, yawn
6. lawful, awful

3 Long and Short Vowels

1.	breathe breath	4.	scrap scrape
2.	bathe bath	5.	gripe grip
3.	tap tape	6.	twin twine

4 Putting Words in Order

1. Mr. Clark couldn't go to sleep.
2. First he tried counting sheep.
3. Then he fixed himself a cup of tea.
4. He still couldn't fall asleep.
5. The next day he was fired for sleeping on the job.

Lesson 12

1 About the Reading

1. 10,000
2. a. queen lays eggs
   b. workers build hives, get food, and care for the young
   c. drones mate with the queen
3. queen and workers
4. drone
5. worker
6. in the fall
7. Drones mate with the queen so she can produce worker eggs.
8. They starve to death.
9. It would not survive because the queen couldn't lay worker eggs.

2 Word Sounds

1. brands   glands
   glands
   lands
2. buck   suck
   suck
   tuck
3. dive   hive
   five
   hive
4. gives   gives
   lives

5. fly   fly
   shy
   try
6. ground   pound
   pound
   round
7. honey   honey
   money
8. Drunks   Skunks
   Punks
   Skunks

3 Words That End in -y

1. sleepy
2. watery
3. sticky
4. corny
5. creepy
6. worthy

1. spicy
2. shiny
3. noisy
4. bouncy
5. flaky
6. wavy

1. sunny
2. snappy
3. piggy
4. kitty
5. buddy
6. foggy

4 Words That End in -ly

1. brotherly
2. calmly
3. nearly
4. sharply
5. bravely
6. weekly
7. barely
8. lonely
9. cheaply
10. commonly

5 Common Sayings

1. bat
2. bee
3. gold
4. lark
5. the nose on your face
6. beet
7. snail
8. fox
9. sheet
10. kite

Lesson 13

1 About the Reading

1. a. He looks at the slant.
   b. He studies the direction of the writing line.
   c. He studies the size and width of the letters.
2. a. false   d. false
   b. true   e. false
   c. true   f. true
3. a. Answers will vary.
   b. Answers will vary.
   c. Answers will vary.
   d. Answers will vary.
4. Answers will vary.
5. Answers will vary.

2 Words That Mean the Same

1. employer
2. large
3. barely
4. allow
5. bright
6. certain
7. present
8. double
9. marry
10. scream

3 Word Opposites

1. asleep
2. sunny
3. birth
4. uphill
5. bright
6. begin
7. won
8. young
9. yesterday
10. summer

4 Vowel Sounds

Star	Air	Ear
1. are	1. bear	1. beer
2. carve	2. fair	2. dear
3. hard	3. stare	3. deer
4. heart	4. their	4. here
5. march	5. wear	5. peer

Lesson 14

1 About the Reading

1. 1863
2. a. They had nowhere to go.
   b. They had nothing to live on.
   c. They had no background in looking out for themselves.
   d. They had nothing to work with.
3. The crowd wasn't prepared to handle all the rain and the ex-slaves didn't know what to do with their freedom.
4. Answers will vary.

2 Choosing the Right Heading

Farms	Baseball	Soups	War
Games	School	Lights	Christmas
Snacks	Water		

3 Words That End in -er

1. sticker
2. hanger
3. heater
4. cracker
5. mower
1. miner
2. diver
3. maker
4. dancer
5. freezer
1. trapper
2. batter
3. dipper
4. zipper
5. swimmer

4 More Words That End in -er

1. coaster
2. dresser
3. folder
4. rubber
5. campers
6. slippers
7. corner
8. lighter
9. poker
10. checkers

5 Putting Sentences in Order

1. When I was fifteen years old, I was put up on the block for sale.
2. A white man was there who was very rich and mean and owned many slaves.
3. He was so mean that many white and black people hated him.
4. When he bid for me, I talked right out on the block.
5. "If you bid for me, I will take a knife and cut myself from ear to ear before I would be owned by you."

Lesson 15

1 About the Reading

1. Hold Fast, Saw Tooth, Wrap Around, Brink Twist, Necktie (any three)
2. He gold-plated them and sold them to a big store.
3. Their main goal is to own at least one strand of every kind of barbed wire ever made.
4. a. The doctor gets into his helicopter.
   b. He flies over miles of fence looking for barbed wire.
   c. He sees something that looks good.
   d. He sets his helicopter down in a field.
   e. He takes out his wire cutters and snips off a strand.
5. the way they looked.
6. farmers
7. They used it to keep cattle away from their crops.

2 Words That Rhyme

1. cold, gold, folded, sold
2. brink, drink, sink, stink
3. tent, bent, went, rent
4. Mack, rack, lacked, sack
5. cared, share, bare, spare
6. Sutter, utter, cutters, butter
7. tucked, stuck, sucked, luck
8. king, bring, sting, sing
9. wiped, griped, swiped, ripe
10. crook, look, hook, book

3 How Do You Say It?

1. flock
2. loaf
3. deck
4. pack
5. pot
6. herd
7. school
8. batch
9. bunch
10. quart
11. pair
12. can
13. bar
14. book
15. load

Review: Lessons 1-15

1 Choosing the Answer

1. sticky
2. flaky
3. foggy
4. repaid
5. filed
6. crosses
7. nowhere
8. grouches
9. batter
10. bid
11. grape
12. drones
13. Fourth of July
14. North and South

2 Silent Letters

1. wrote
2. dumb
3. badge
4. Dutch
5. young
6. build
7. knee
8. dodge
9. batch
10. writer
11. witch
12. certain

3 Matching

1. rainbow
2. oven
3. mower
4. towel
5. fence
6. stamp
7. alphabet
8. piggy
9. wax
10. pepper

4 Word Sounds

1. whose
2. certain
3. allow
4. bath
5. soup
6. heading
7. flood
8. ginger

5 Compound Words

1. lipstick
2. babysitter
3. sunglasses
4. ashtray
5. firecrackers
6. overdone
7. stagecoach
8. cheesecake
9. underline
10. busybody

Lesson 16

1 About the Reading

1.

	Fish	Whales
a. Breathing	in the water	out of the water
b. Blood	cold-blooded	warm-blooded
c. Birth	lay eggs	young are born alive

2. Cold-blooded means the temperature of the blood changes as the temperature of the environment changes.
3. Warm-blooded means the temperature of the blood stays the same even when the temperature of the environment changes.
4. a. true
   b. true
   c. false
   d. true
   e. false
   f. false
   g. true
   h. true
   i. false
   j. true
   k. true
5. Answers will vary. Frequently such animals are declared endangered species and killing them is forbidden.

2 Changing the y to i

1. busier — busiest
2. noisier — noisiest
3. happier — happiest
4. luckier — luckiest
5. sleepier — sleepiest

3 Changing the y to i

1. happily
2. busily
3. noisily
4. sleepily
5. Luckily

4 Silly Little Stories

1. swear, sweater, sweat, swell
2. lot, lost, locked, loss
3. Dan, dam, dashed, damp
4. band, bank, bang, banker
5. crust, crushed (or crunched), crumbs, crunched (or crushed)
6. witch, without, wished, wings, winked

5 Which Word Fits Best?

1. people
2. mammal
3. find
4. horses
5. flower
6. football
7. cow
8. wood
9. tomorrow
10. hardly ever

Lesson 17

1 About the Reading

1. Charles
2. eight years
3. more than thirty
4. teaching
5. about two thousand dollars
6. He intended only to scare the driver.
7. a. He made careful plans.
   b. He always worked alone.
   c. He never held up stagecoaches near home.
   d. He never told anyone about his plans.
8. A teacher earned about one thousand dollars.
9. Answers may vary.

2 Words That Mean the Same

1. limbs
2. bold
3. earn
4. clue
5. robbery
6. alive
7. all right
8. cause
9. high-class
10. ton

3 Word Opposites

1. under
2. dozed
3. scared
4. full
5. awful
6. harmful
7. leave
8. fresh
9. froze
10. cool

4 The Ending -ful

1. successful
2. truthful
3. mouthful
4. thoughtful
5. sinful
6. cupful
7. forgetful
8. hopeful
9. wasteful
10. spiteful

5 A Verse from Black Bart

This is the way I get my money and <u>bread</u>.
    When I have a <u>chance</u>, why should I refuse it?
I'll not need either when I'm <u>dead</u>,
    And I only tax those who are <u>able</u> to lose it.
So <u>blame</u> me not for what I've done,
    I don't deserve your <u>curses</u>.
And if for some cause I must be <u>hung</u>,
    Let it be for my <u>verses</u>.

Lesson 18

1 About the Reading

1. The earth is more than two billion years old.
2. They can tell the age of the rocks that make up the earth's crust.
3. The heavy matter in the center of the earth is liquid iron.
4. Life began in the ocean.
5. a. The earth was a ball of hot whirling gases.
   b. The gases began to turn into liquid form.
   c. The outer shell of the earth changed from liquid to solid.
   d. The rains fell.
   e. Oceans and seas filled with water.
   f. One-celled forms came into being.
   g. Worms and starfish came into being.

2 Word Sounds

1. sprinted, spray, sprawled, sprained
2. stranger, strong, streets, strike
3. swung, swiftly, swimming, switch
4. scraped, screen, screamed, scrubbing
5. squirrel, squeezed, square, squirt

3 The Ending -less

1. sleeveless
2. breathless
3. sleepless
4. worthless
5. thoughtless
6. meatless
7. cloudless
8. useless
9. hairless
10. Needless

4 Same or Opposite?

1. same
2. same
3. same
4. opposite
5. opposite
6. same
7. same
8. opposite
9. opposite
10. same
11. opposite
12. same
13. opposite
14. opposite

5 Spelling Check

1. March
2. crown
3. universe
4. stork
5. January
6. nerve
7. iron
8. drone
9. rainbow
10. cheese

Lesson 19

1 About the Reading

1. a. They used galleys to guard the coast.
   b. They used galleys to remove ships wounded in battle.
2. Note: The details below may be listed in any order. Other details may be included as well.
   a. The galley was mainly an open boat for four hundred men.
   b. Convicts manned the oars that made the galley move swiftly.
   c. Each oar was manned by five convicts.
   d. Sometimes the convicts rowed for twenty-four hours without any rest.

e. Nobody ever washed.

3. a. They would work at their respective trades.
   b. They would get some food from the nearest town.
   c. They would get much needed sleep.

4. They used steam when it became available because it was faster.

2 Words That Sound the Same

1. be, bee
2. know, no
3. Ann, an
4. thrown, throne
5. cent, sent
6. cell, sell
7. hear, here
8. where, wear

3 Which Word Does Not Fit?

1. question
2. dry
3. person
4. hidden
5. soap
6. work
7. one-half
8. port
9. dirt
10. gripe
11. bumped into
12. water

4 Words That Begin with *un-*

1. unmated
2. untie
3. unmade
4. unarmed
5. unfriendly
6. unsafe
7. undress
8. unable
9. unfolded
10. unfair

5 Common Sayings

1. good
2. old
3. will
4. hatched
5. away
6. ton
7. play
8. heard
9. worth
10. thousand
11. heart
12. Home

Lesson 20

1 About the Reading

1. February 11
2. February 22
3. bodyguard
4. swearing
5. New York City
6. 2 terms
7. 1789
8. He was the first president of the United States. He commanded the Continental Army in its effort to gain independence from England. He also served as president of the convention that wrote the Constitution.
9. four years
10. the one dollar bill

2 Vowel Sounds

1. born, barn, burned
2. crook, crack, creaking
3. time, tame, team
4. slum, slim, slammed
5. truck, trick, track
6. slung, sling, slang
7. peeled, pail, pile
8. store, stared, stars
9. While, wheel, whale
10. drank, drinks, drunk

3 The Ending -*ly*

1. nearly
2. Surely
3. hardly
4. swiftly
5. lovely
6. really
7. badly
8. friendly

4 Compound Words

1. body + guard
2. country + men
3. check + book
4. every + where
5. cat + fish
6. busy + body
7. police + man
8. some + one
9. in + land
10. hide + out
11. under + line
12. star + fish

5 More Common Sayings

1. flies
2. boils
3. put, basket
4. wool
5. back
6. say
7. friend
8. hole
9. pod
10. candy, baby
11. speak
12. easy

Review: Lessons 1-20

1 Twenty Questions

1. George Washington
2. February
3. Fourth of July
4. Mayflower
5. galley
6. scribes
7. El Dorado
8. California
9. forty-niners
10. warm-blooded
11. cold-blooded
12. quarts
13. pints
14. ounces
15. alphabet
16. B.C.
17. Pinocchio
18. bigwig
19. drone
20. New Year's Day

2 Words That Mean the Same

1. nearly
2. bold
3. munch
4. deserve
5. rim
6. buddy
7. present
8. guide
9. cause
10. utter
11. slim
12. worthless

3 Word Opposites

1. simple
2. remember
3. thaw
4. shrank
5. deadly
6. spiteful
7. ugly
8. spicy
9. certain
10. overdone
11. bold
12. crooked

4 Which Word Fits Best?

1. peep
2. hour
3. chew
4. writing
5. cross
6. oars
7. gills
8. firecracker
9. March is to February
10. water is to ice

5 Words That Sound the Same

1. through
2. be
3. sent
4. weak
5. thrown
6. bored
7. cents
8. weigh
9. brake
10. know

Book 3

Lesson 1

1 About the Story

1. Steven drives a van for a living.
2. He has had this job for five years.
3. His sister's name is Ruth.
4. Steven sees Ruth once a week, on Thursday night.
5. a. The exercise class would help Steven feel more relaxed.
   b. The class would also give him an opportunity to meet new people.
6. At first, Steven gets angry.
7. At the end of the story, Steven decides to give the class a try.
8. A pact is an agreement or bargain.
9. Answers may vary. Ruth may be encouraging Steven to "get out more, do things and meet some new people" because she enjoys these activities. On the other hand, Steven does visit her every Thursday and she may be trying to prevent him from getting into a rut like she has.
10. Ruth tells Steven that he is still young, and he has been driving a van for five years. Therefore he is probably in his mid-twenties.

2 The Ending -ing

1. blessing
2. building
3. clearing
4. dressing
5. stuffing
6. washing

1. bathing
2. lining
3. paving
4. wiring
5. coming
6. icing

1. bedding
2. clipping
3. fitting
4. cutting
5. padding
6. wedding

3 How Do These People Earn a Living?

1. teacher
2. baker
3. farmer
4. fiddler
5. miner
6. waiter
7. boxer
8. manager
9. teller
10. lawyer

4 Compound Words

1. road + work
2. side + walk
3. tool + box
4. rose + bud
5. back + fire
6. dish + pan
7. pig + pen
8. man + kind
9. home + made
10. news + paper

Lesson 2

1 About the Story

1. Steven's best friend is Jerome.
2. Steven is taking a yoga class at the Y.M.C.A.
3. He wandered into the yoga class by mistake.
4. Jerome thinks yoga has stranger exercises.
5. Jerome didn't laugh at Steven for taking the yoga class.
6. Jerome seems to have let himself into Steven's apartment, and he helps himself to the stew Steven has made for dinner.

2 Adding -est to Words

1. finest
2. rudest
3. nicest
4. latest
5. ripest
6. sorest

1. proudest
2. shortest
3. cheapest
4. greatest
5. meanest
6. highest

1. saddest
2. biggest
3. thinnest
4. dimmest
5. maddest
6. hottest

3 How Do These People Earn a Living?

1. reporter
2. carpenter
3. bodyguard
4. actor
5. tailor
6. babysitter
7. trainer
8. clown
9. shortstop
10. fisherman
11. scribe
12. doctor

4 Compound Words

1. pay + check
2. tooth + paste
3. under + stand
4. corn + starch
5. chalk + board
6. short + cake
7. class + room
8. under + shirt
9. flash + light
10. cook + book
11. work + shop
12. hand + shake

Lesson 3

1 About the Story

1. Jerome hadn't been in a library for twelve years.
2. All Jerome ever did in the library was flirt with the girls.
3. She said she thought he belonged in a reform school.
4. He wanted to find out more about yoga because he wanted to talk Steven out of taking a yoga class.

5. At first Jerome thought yoga was yogurt.
6. The ladies are pleasant, smiling at him when he almost knocks over the flag.
7. He feels awful while in the library even though no one is giving him a hard time.
8. A vow is a promise.
9. Going to the library brings back bad memories of being kicked out of the high school library, but Jerome signs out the book on yoga without incident.

2 **Adding -y to Words**

1. tasty	1. grouchy	1. runny
2. shaky	2. stuffy	2. doggy
3. shady	3. bossy	3. patty
4. stony	4. rainy	4. knotty
5. edgy	5. squeaky	5. woolly

3 **Who Uses What?**

1. flashlight
2. punch
3. towel
4. ashtray
5. folder
6. oars
7. notebook
8. sponge
9. Bible
10. charm
11. jet
12. buggies

4 **Compound Words**

1. black + board	7. sun + light
2. ear + ring	8. suit + case
3. house + wife	9. eye + strain
4. fruit + cake	10. ring + side
5. over + grown	11. bob + sled
6. grown + up	12. free + way

Lesson 4

1 **About the Story**

1. Jerome was studying up on yoga.
2. It is a way to relax and free oneself from the phony nonsense in this world. He also tells her that some people claim it improves their sex life.
3. Jerome says he always goes to her place.
4. a. She is waiting for a call from her new manager.
   b. Jerome's place looks like a pigpen.
5. Ginger hangs up on Jerome.
6. Jerome won't stop clowning around.
7. Answers will vary.

2 **Changing the y to i**

1. grouchier	grouchiest
2. rainier	rainiest
3. icier	iciest
4. stuffier	stuffiest
5. bossier	bossiest
6. rosier	rosiest

3 **The Ending -y**

trashy	1. hairy	salty	6. brainy
bloody	2. jumpy	brainy	7. salty
hairy	3. puffy	tricky	8. bloody
jumpy	4. risky	puffy	9. tricky
risky	5. trashy	woody	10. Woody

4 **Who Uses What?**

1. iron	6. putty
2. leash	7. globe
3. grill	8. gloves
4. plow	9. platter
5. spices	10. sails

5 **Compound Words**

1. rail + road	5. dream + land
2. basket + ball	6. grand + father
3. under + ground	7. cheap + skate
4. grand + mother	8. wood + pecker

Lesson 5

1 **About the Story**

1. It got you thinking about what kinds of information the story might contain.
2. She sang with a band, wrote songs and gave voice lessons.
3. She had met Jerome six months ago in a hardware store.
4. Jerome worked as a clerk in the hardware store.
5. Ginger was in love with Jerome.
6. No one knows for sure how Jerome felt about Ginger.
7. Ginger's mother thought her daughter's apartment didn't look at all homey.
8. Ginger had not told her mother how wealthy she was.
9. Answers will vary.

2 **The Ending -ly**

lately	1. properly	wildly	6. costly
madly	2. shyly	oddly	7. lately
truthfully	3. truthfully	costly	8. lively
peacefully	4. madly	shyly	9. peacefully
properly	5. wildly	lively	10. Oddly

3 **Words That Mean the Same**

1. plead	5. frighten	9. beginning
2. brink	6. notice	10. dense
3. edgy	7. bright	11. pledge
4. shove	8. gaze	12. healthy

4 **Compound Words**

1. tooth + brush	6. bill + fold
2. Thanks + giving	7. snow + ball
3. over + board	8. snap + shot
4. gum + drop	9. high + way
5. flower + pot	10. cross + walk

Lesson 6

1 About the Story
1. This story takes place in the hardware store.
2. It is evening.
3. a. Ginger might stop being angry with him.
   b. It might encourage her to paint her apartment.
4. The lid came off, and paint spilled all over Jerome, the counter, and the floor.
5. Tony laughed very hard.
6. It took seven hours to clean up the mess.
7. Answers may vary. The first paragraph of the story suggests that Jerome wants to take the paint now and perhaps pay for it when he gets his next paycheck.
8. Answers may vary.

2 The Ending -ly
freshly	1. neatly	rarely	6. squarely
hourly	2. rarely	squarely	7. mildly
neatly	3. hourly	successfully	8. tightly
tightly	4. certainly	mildly	9. thickly
thickly	5. freshly	certainly	10. successfully

3 Word Opposites
1. hairy	5. rarely	9. tense
2. costly	6. skinny	10. risky
3. grownup	7. ugly	11. loose
4. frozen	8. phony	12. dumb

4 Compound Words
1. dish + rag	5. over + head
2. finger + nail	6. drug + store
3. tail + spin	7. finger + print
4. any + more	8. in + side

Lesson 7

1 About the Story
1. Steven had a slight cold and apparently wasn't feeling too well.
2. He was catching on to the yoga exercises quite quickly.
3. Holly asked Steven if he wanted to go out for a cup of coffee.
4. The sugar in it could make people grouchy, restless, fat, and unhealthy.
5. He apparently has decided not to order the chocolate cake when he says, "Well, so much for the chocolate cake."
6. Steven learned that yoga is a whole way of life. He also learned that in becoming involved with yoga he had a lot more to think about than he imagined he would.
7. a. Steven's apartment
   b. The Y.M.C.A.
   c. a coffee shop

2 The Endings -ful and -less
A.		B.	
restless		1.	stressful
stressful		2.	tasteless
sugarless		3.	harmful
spotless		4.	armful
armful		5.	peaceful
peaceful		6.	restless
harmful		7.	spotless
tasteless		8.	sugarless

3 Same or Opposite?
1. opposite	7. opposite
2. opposite	8. same
3. same	9. opposite
4. same	10. same
5. same	11. opposite
6. same	12. same

4 Compound Words
1. knock + out	6. door + knob
2. ship + wreck	7. rest + room
3. life + guard	8. come + back
4. match + book	9. eye + sight
5. light + house	10. knee + cap

Lesson 8

1 About the Story
1. This story takes place in Ginger's apartment.
2. It probably takes place in the morning since Ginger was fixing breakfast.
3. Gail wanted to stay at Ginger's for a day or two.
4. Gail goes to see her parents only when she wants money.
5. She had banged her head against the front door.
6. Ginger suggested that Gail ought to think about how she is treating her parents.
7. We know that Gail doesn't live with her parents because the story said she visited them only when she wanted money.
8. Probably most students will feel that Gail is not treating her parents very well and that she should be more considerate.

2 The Endings -ful and -less
A.		B.	
countless		1.	homeless
faithful		2.	spoonful
homeless		3.	sunless
joyful		4.	faithful
painful		5.	painful
painless		6.	watchful
spoonful		7.	joyful
sunless		8.	countless
watchful		9.	painless
worthless		10.	worthless

3 Same or Opposite?

1. opposite	5. opposite	9. same
2. same	6. opposite	10. opposite
3. same	7. same	11. opposite
4. same	8. opposite	12. same

4 Compound Words

1. coffeecake	5. scoreboard	9. crybaby
2. newsstand	6. waistline	10. kinfolks
3. washcloth	7. leapfrog	11. cheapskate
4. meatballs	8. pitchfork	12. spendthrift

Lesson 9

1 About the Story

1. Jerome was feeling lousy because he hadn't heard from Ginger in four weeks.
2. At first, Jerome thought Ginger was calling him.
3. Jerome wasn't pleased.
4. Steven spoke sharply, indicating he was angry.
5. Steven had called Jerome to invite him to Holly's party.
6. Going to Holly's party was better than sitting in a bar by himself.
7. Jerome is disappointed at first. At the end of the phone call, he is glad to be going to Holly's party rather than sitting in a bar by himself.
8. Probably the most obvious answer is that Jerome won't call a woman after they've had an argument. Instead, he waits for her to call him.
9. Answers will vary.

2 The Ending -en

1. frozen	7. weaken
2. forgiven	8. written
3. sunken	9. threaten
4. forgotten	10. loosen
5. broken	11. moisten
6. chosen	12. mistaken

3 Which Word Does Not Fit?

1. buddy	6. speak
2. ice cubes	7. worm
3. blouse	8. trip
4. chocolate cake	9. breathing
5. beef	10. play

Lesson 10

1 About the Story

1. a. Finding a parking place was difficult.
   b. The machines might not work properly.
   c. You have to be careful not to lose anything.
2. Holly was writing "Out of Order" signs for the machines that didn't work.
3. Holly had tried two washing machines.
4. a. The four quarters and two dimes ($1.20) she lost suggests she tried two machines — sixty cents in each machine.
   b. She was writing two "Out of Order" signs.
5. Since she had hung up on him, he felt she should phone him to apologize.
6. Jerome wants to see her, so he should call her.
7. Jerome wasn't taking any steps to get what he wanted.
8. Answers may vary.

2 The Ending -en

1. driven	5. bitten	9. given
2. fallen	6. eaten	10. ridden
3. shaken	7. spoken	11. Risen
4. straightened	8. beaten	12. rotten

3 Which Word Does Not Fit?

1. newspaper	5. pest	9. ivy
2. month	6. drum	10. season
3. deck	7. saucepan	11. whale
4. building	8. highway	12. Rome

4 Spelling Check

1. breakfast	6. coffee
2. alphabet	7. wedding
3. mammal	8. mirror
4. Christmas	9. Swiss
5. doctor	10. thirteen

Lesson 11

1 About the Story

1. a. Ginger had had her phone taken out.
   b. She had gone camping.
2. She was daydreaming about never having to work again.
3. a. She is going to buy a phone for every room.
   b. She is going to paint her walls.
   c. She is going to read all the newspapers she can find.
4. Life in the city looks safer than camping in the woods.
5. Ginger had gone camping to perk herself up after her trouble with Jerome. When she thought she heard a growling sound, she became scared and ran away as fast as she could.
6. Answers will vary.
7. Answers will vary.

2 Words That Begin with re-

1. react	6. recall
2. refuse	7. recover
3. remarks	8. repeat
4. respect	9. rejected, rejection
5. reveal	10. require

3 Words That Mean the Same
1. lousy   6. faithful
2. respond   7. juicy
3. boast   8. require
4. rejoice   9. recall
5. nervous   10. mistaken

4 What Is Where?

A Laundromat	A Library	A Diner
1. bleach	1. bookshelves	1. grill
2. coin machines	2. newspapers	2. oven
3. dryers	3. records	3. tips

5 What Is Where?

A Circus	A Concert	A Baseball Game
1. clowns	1. drums	1. center field
2. dancing bears	2. flutes	2. pitchers
3. side shows	3. stage	3. scoreboards

Lesson 12

1 About the Story
1. Steven's boss had given him the free passes.
2. The Colts and the Cowboys were playing.
3. a. She asked if they could sit behind the batter's box.
   b. She didn't recognize the coach.
   (Note: The story contains additional evidence that Holly doesn't know anything about football.)
4. When the man next to Steven bumped him, the popcorn spilled, landing on his coat and trousers.
5. "The Star-Spangled Banner" is played.
6. Holly probably knows a little about baseball. She knows the term *batter's box*, but doesn't seem to realize it is associated only with baseball.
7. Answers will vary.

2 Words That Begin with *re-*
1. revive   7. retired
2. remove   8. related
3. report   9. recovery
4. repair   10. return
5. refreshed   11. retreat
6. reduce   12. reply

3 Word Opposites
1. forgive   6. fallen
2. wilt   7. scratchy
3. nervous   8. listen
4. moldy   9. sunless
5. reveal   10. wasteful

4 Compound Words
1. footprint   5. homesick   9. blacktop
2. quarterback   6. daybreak   10. courtroom
3. eggshell   7. standstill   11. lukewarm
4. deadline   8. wastebasket   12. playground

Lesson 13

1 About the Story
1. Jerome thought it would be a way to see Ginger.
2. Tony was supposed to invite Ginger to the party.
3. a. He got rid of the cockroaches in the kitchen.
   b. He swept the cobwebs from his bookshelves and ceiling.
   c. He cleaned the carpet.
4. Jerome's party really started at ten o'clock.
5. It ended at four in the morning.
6. Ginger never arrived. Everyone else had a great time and didn't notice that Jerome was miserable.
7. Answers will vary.

2 Words That Begin with *in-*
1. inhale   6. instruct
2. invent   7. inquire
3. invade   8. infect
4. invite   9. intend
5. increase   10. inspire

3 Which Word Fits Best?
1. chirp   5. look down upon   9. stale
2. neck   6. lung   10. present
3. Boston   7. land   11. roar
4. coffeecake   8. steam   12. year

4 Consonants
1. gŭt • ter   6. cŭt • ting
2. măt • ter   7. măm • mal
3. sŭm • mer   8. căt • ty
4. hăp • pen   9. pĕp • per
5. mŭg • ger   10. slĭp • per

Lesson 14

1 About the Story
1. He didn't get along with her very well. He stayed in a motel during the week and came home on weekends only to see his children.
2. Mrs. Darkpill began to cut down Tony's chestnut tree. He tried without success to talk some sense into her.
3. She complained that he had whipped her daughter.
4. Her name seems most fitting. Her personality is far from cheerful.
5. Answers will vary.

2 The *gh* and *ght* Words
1. might, right
2. right
3. neighbor, sighed
4. ought, daughters
5. dough, rough, cough, tough
6. sleigh, height, eight, bright
7. enough

3 Same or Opposite

1. opposite
2. same
3. same
4. opposite
5. opposite
6. opposite
7. same
8. same
9. opposite
10. same
11. same
12. opposite

4 Double Consonants

1. stŭt • ter
2. clŭt • ter
3. bĭt • ten
4. wrăp • per
5. thĭn • ner
6. hĭt • ter
7. lŏb • by
8. shăt • ter
9. trăp • per
10. cŏm • mon

Lesson 15

1 About the Story

1. Ginger is parked in front of her driveway.
2. She accuses him of having girls in until all hours of the night.
3. coffee
4. booze
5. Ginger puts her arm around Mrs. Darkpill to lead her to the couch.
6. The neighbors, hearing the uproar, called the police.
7. Students will probably agree.
8. Answers will vary.

2 The ea and ear Words

1. beard, heart, feared, head
2. repeated, nearby, pleaded, freak
3. leather, dread, feather, mincemeat
4. mean, cheap, headed, beach
5. heard, beard, dreadful, preach
6. beat, sea, leap

3 Syllables

1. card • board
2. bright • ly
3. cheer • ful
4. sub • way
5. proud • ly
6. in • hale
7. un • clear
8. stair • way
9. cob • web
10. fair • ness
11. sad • ness
12. in • vade

4 More Work with Units

1. months
2. hours
3. seconds
4. quarts
5. ounces
6. feet
7. letters
8. rooms
9. states

Lesson 16

1 About the Story

1. a. peanut butter balls
   b. prune whip
   c. date-nut bread
2. Holly was writing a cookbook.
3. peanut butter balls
4. prune whip
5. He complains rather than taking action to make life better.
6. He is living by a set of outdated rules.
7. The bread was burned.
8. Answers may vary.
9. Answers may vary.

2 The Sounds for ow

1. flowerpot
2. bowling
3. bowl
4. crowbar
5. scarecrows
6. pillow
7. elbow
8. shower
9. grownups
10. towel rack
11. rowboat
12. cow

3 Syllables

1. yesterday
2. woodpecker
3. Cinderella
4. helicopter
5. laundromat
6. recipe
7. hangover
8. thrifty

4 Brain Benders

1. false
2. true
3. false
4. true
5. true
6. true
7. true
8. false
9. false
10. false

Lesson 17

1 About the Story

1. a. Tony's apartment
   b. a diner
   c. a men's clothing store
2. Mr. Dennis is Tony's boss.
3. Since Mr. Dennis answered the phone in an "extremely unfriendly voice," we can assume he was in a bad mood.
4. Tony tells Mr. Dennis that he is coming down with the flu.
5. He decides to check out the sale at a men's clothing store.
6. Mr. Dennis sees Tony at the store when he is supposed to be home sick.
7. Answers will vary.
8. Answers will vary.

2 Sounds for ow

1. dishtowel
2. landowner
3. blowout
4. snowplow
5. washbowl
6. townspeople
7. downpour
8. wildflowers
9. showoff
10. lowdown

3 Which Word Does Not Fit?

1. peas
2. unfriendly
3. knees
4. purse
5. weak
6. rain
7. shelter
8. relax
9. nervous
10. destroy
11. conceal
12. mute

4 Syllables

1. con • fess
2. booth
3. ex • treme
4. ex • treme • ly
5. shop • per
6. flu
7. six • teen
8. yes • ter • day
9. win • ner
10. pay • day
11. home • sick
12. rest • room
13. o • ver • board
14. un • friend • ly
15. bas • ket • ball

Lesson 18

1 About the Story

1. Steven thinks Jerome can't admit when he's made a mistake and take the initiative to straighten out things with Ginger.
2. Steven is trying to get Jerome to understand that he will have to take some action in order to get what he wants out of life.
3. Jerome thinks Ginger might have started the fight with Tony's neighbor just to get out of going to his party.
4. Jerome only complains and won't do anything to get back together with Ginger.
5. Jerome seems to decide Steven is right. Evidence of this is Jerome's deciding to call Ginger.

2 Short Stories

1. discussed, expands, disagreed, extra, convince
2. exceeding, exchanged, unfriendly, unfit, extra
3. exhausted, uncertain, unhealthy, expenses, income

3 Who Uses What?

Baker
1. cake pans
2. dough
3. oven
4. pie plates
5. rolling pin

Barber
1. chair
2. clippers
3. comb
4. mirror
5. shaving cream

Carpenter
1. boards
2. drill
3. hammer
4. nails
5. saws

Fisherman
1. bait
2. boat
3. hooks
4. net
5. rod

4 Spelling Check

1. thumb
2. August
3. wallet
4. paycheck
5. potato
6. Cinderella
7. waltz
8. cheapskate

Lesson 19

1 About the Story

1. Jerome decides to go see her rather than calling her.
2. Most of the story takes place at the nightclub where Ginger is singing.
3. Ginger is sitting next to the piano player when Jerome first sees her.
4. At first, Jerome tells Ginger he came to see her because he wanted to hear her sing "September Song."
5. Ginger threatens to have the bouncer throw Jerome out of the club.
6. Ginger touches Jerome gently on the cheek and goes to sing "September Song."

2 Months of the Year

1. January
2. December
3. December
4. November
5. February
6. Answer will vary
7. September (or August)
8. June (or May)
9. March
10. June
11. September
12. December
13. Answer will vary
14. Answer will vary

3 The Four Seasons

Spring
1. April
2. Easter
3. flowers blooming
4. spring training

Summer
1. August
2. beach
3. Fourth of July
4. the All-Star game

Autumn
1. falling leaves
2. October
3. schools open
4. Thanksgiving

Winter
1. Christmas
2. December
3. ice skating
4. snow storms

4 Twelve Questions

1. upstairs
2. indoors
3. infield
4. income
5. disposing
6. overdone
7. content
8. included
9. overlook
10. replying
11. request
12. deflate

Lesson 20

1 About the Story

1. Holly is giving a party to celebrate signing a contract for her cookbook.
2. Jerome asked Holly if he could bring anything to the party.
3. Holly is sick of all the health food she had to eat while testing recipes for her cookbook.
4. about midnight
5. She had to sing at the nightclub.
6. prune whip
7. chocolate cheesecake
8. Ginger likes the people from the yoga class.
9. Jerome is happy for a change.
10. Jerome seems to have learned that life has its ups and downs, and a person never knows what will happen next.

2 Compound Words

1. passport
2. Passover
3. homebody
4. backpack
5. backbone
6. firetrap
7. dishpan
8. drumstick
9. teaspoons
10. overalls

3 Words That Mean the Same

1. find
2. tired
3. overweight
4. hardly
5. hurled
6. rough
7. lance
8. wander
9. singe
10. pout

4 Word Opposites

1. female
2. sour
3. morning
4. heat
5. freeze
6. crawl
7. common
8. bored
9. certain
10. contract

5 Feelings

1. cheered. The fans were happy to see a member of the opposing team thrown out of the game for unsportsmanlike behavior.
2. excited. At last, Joan could apply for a job that really appealed to her.
3. angry. He had gotten nothing for his quarter.
4. overcome with feeling. Charles's emotions reflected his happiness at winning the money.
5. rejected. John felt his neighbor didn't want him at the party.
6. happy. His boss's leaving would remove that source of irritation.
7. thankful. She was very aware of how fortunate she was to have her son found unharmed.
8. Answers will vary.

Review: Lessons 1-20

1 Word Study

1. c
2. b
3. d
4. a
5. b
6. b
7. a
8. c
9. a
10. c
11. d
12. a
13. a
14. c
15. d

2 Words That Mean the Same

1. loyal
2. fussy
3. nervous
4. fib
5. poor
6. beg
7. content
8. hoist
9. grab
10. pledge

3 Word Opposites

1. straight
2. spotless
3. shrink
4. quiet
5. underneath
6. fancy
7. complex
8. loosen
9. phony
10. costly

4 Syllables

1. cloud • less
2. suc • cess • ful
3. rob • ber
4. side • ways
5. thir • teen
6. thought • ful
7. re • tire
8. hand • shake
9. sit • ter
10. peace • ful • ly

5 Word Sounds

1. walk
2. city
3. gentle
4. great
5. good
6. plow
7. could
8. certain

6 Spelling Check

1. courtroom
2. highway
3. England
4. eggshell
5. school
6. ear
7. cookbook
8. ashtray
9. kitchen
10. El Dorado

Answer: cheesecake

Book 4

Lesson 1

1 About the Reading

1. a. true   f. false
   b. false   g. true
   c. true   h. true
   d. false   i. false
   e. true   j. false

2. The person is putting a strain on his heart by making it beat harder and faster.
3. 1,660,000 people in the U.S. die from heart disease.
4. Answers may vary.

2 The Human Body

1. artery
2. vein
3. nose
4. brain
5. elbow
6. bloodstream
7. nerve
8. ribs
9. lungs
10. spleen

3 Adding -er

1. dealer
2. reader
3. blender
4. printer
5. performer

1. trader
2. shaker
3. hiker
4. liner
5. believer

1. runner
2. drummer
3. bidder
4. flipper
5. patter

4 Syllables

1. book • case
2. win • ner
3. strong • ly
4. clut • ter
5. lo • cate
6. hope • less
7. nor • mal
8. for • give
9. cop • per
10. per • form

5 Brain Benders

1. kind
2. want something badly
3. a snob
4. full of pride
5. strongly moved
6. agree with your friend
7. insist on having your own way
8. teasing you
9. hurts your feelings
10. angry

Lesson 2

1 About the Reading

1. Baltimore
2. a reform school
3. the Boston Red Sox
4. Yankee Stadium
5. fifteen years
6. His legs gave out.
7. cancer
8. 53
9. Answers may vary. The reading suggests he lacked self-discipline and maturity — particularly as evidenced by the way he managed money.

2 Games and Sports

1. quarterback
2. outfield
3. yards
4. bases
5. squares
6. height
7. racket
8. paddle
9. checkers
10. dice

3 Words That Mean the Same

1. perform
2. car
3. brag
4. normal
5. gloomy
6. conceal
7. wrong
8. message
9. trousers
10. female

4 Word Opposites

1. conclude
2. edge
3. built
4. dull
5. normal
6. increase
7. restless
8. smooth
9. plump
10. brand-new

5 The Ending -er

1. buzzer
2. jumper
3. killer
4. learner
5. broiler
6. strainer

1. wiper
2. insider
3. outsider
4. invader
5. tuner
6. breather

1. digger
2. gunner
3. logger
4. jogger
5. skipper
6. snapper

6 Syllables

1. grāve • yard
2. dĭs • turb
3. wrăp • per
4. ĭn • quīre
5. ŭn • dĭd
6. tĕn • nĭs
7. brĕak • fast
8. fĭd • dle
9. păd • dle
10. trāin • ing

Lesson 3

1 About the Reading

1. *Concept* means a thought or idea about something.
2. They are afraid something serious has happened.
3. "A long time" can be anything from a few days to ten or twenty years.
4. They think "a long time" means thousands of years.
5. They think the person is rude or unfit for his job.
6. The Pueblo Indians begin something when they feel the time is right.
7. He had to wait until 2 a.m. for the dance to start.
8. Different groups of people have different concepts about time.
9. Answers will vary.

2 Time

1. spring, summer, autumn, winter
2. Tuesday, Wednesday, Thursday, Friday
3. dawn, noon, dusk, midnight (or *midnight* may come first)
4. New Year's Day, Easter, Fourth of July, Christmas Eve
5. second, minute, half-hour, hour
6. July, August, September, October
7. day, week, month, year
8. wristwatch, alarm clock, grandfather's clock, sun
9. free time, a normal working day, time and a half, double time

3 More about Time

1. steal
2. earned
3. save
4. waste
5. use
6. spent
7. lost
8. blown
9. lend
10. borrowed

4 The Ending -y

1. soapy
2. dusty
3. sandy
4. curly
5. bushy

1. breezy
2. wheezy
3. scary
4. nervy
5. greasy

1. peppy
2. potty
3. fatty
4. choppy
5. clammy

5 Syllables

1. wrĭst • watch
2. South • wĕst
3. clăm • my
4. short • cŭt
5. ŏb • jĕct
6. breath • less
7. rē • quīre
8. săd • ness
9. hōpe • ful
10. mĭs • trŭst

Lesson 4

1 About the Reading

1. 800,000
2. where it is cold or in salt water
3. Insects have six legs.

4. three
5. feelers
6. They help plants to grow by carrying pollen from one flower to another.
7. a. They serve as food for a number of animals.
   b. They return matter to the soil.
   c. They give us honey, silk, and wax.
8. a. Some bite.
   b. Some sting.
   c. Some carry diseases.
   d. They can mess up kitchens, etc.
   e. Some destroy crops.
   f. Some harm forests.
9. There are fewer insects in colder places.
10. There are so many of them that if they were larger they might overrun an area.

2 Name That Insect or Bug

1. bee
2. termite
3. ladybug
4. spider
5. tick
6. housefly
7. butterfly
8. grasshopper
9. ant
10. cockroach

3 Which Word Fits Best?

1. tick
2. huge
3. ocean
4. orange
5. fish
6. comfort
7. water
8. sand

4 Word Endings

1. speedy
2. rusty
3. silky
4. creamy
5. leafy
6. flowery

1. choosy
2. scaly
3. spongy
4. pasty
5. mousy
6. bony

1. baggy
2. Tommy
3. gummy
4. smoggy
5. floppy
6. sloppy

5 Syllables

1. cŏck • rōach
2. pĭc • nĭc
3. ter • mīte
4. mouth • part
5. ĭn • sĕct
6. pŏl • len
7. flŏp • py
8. cŏn • cĕpt
9. out • look
10. ŭn • lĕss

Lesson 5

1 About the Story

1. dots
2. ten
3. one-third
4. can be unaware of what is happening
5. brain
6. We can be affected by things that we're not even aware of.
7. Subliminal advertising such as this can make us do things we might not do normally.
8. Ads may influence people to buy items they normally would not purchase.

2 Putting Sentences in Order

1. She checks the *TV Guide* to see what time the program is on.
2. She also reads what channel the program is on.
3. She turns on the set. (May also be #1)
4. She turns the knob to the right channel.
5. The picture is not clear at all.
6. She plays with the knobs to get a better picture.
7. The program turns out to be very dull.
8. She falls asleep on the couch.

3 Syllables

1. out • stand • ing
2. un • der • ground
3. yes • ter • day
4. but • ter • fly
5. Wash • ing • ton
6. com • mand • ment
7. grass • hop • per
8. per • form • er
9. re • mem • ber
10. a • part • ment

4 Working with Headings

Spending Time With Friends

Reading	Hiking	Playing Ball
Cooking	Talking on the Phone	Going to Night School
Making Things	Going to a Concert	Going out for Dinner

5 Words That End with -*y*

1. cooky
2. bunny
3. panty
4. battery
5. belly
6. muggy
7. brandy
8. moody
9. bully
10. gravy

Review: Lessons 1-5

1 Answer These Questions

1. vein
2. artery
3. Indian
4. Yankee
5. swamp
6. desert
7. termite
8. grasshopper
9. oxygen
10. carbon dioxide

2 Word Study

1. going on and off
2. a quarter
3. hero
4. George Washington
5. Baltimore
6. United States
7. tennis courts
8. meadow
9. museum
10. the American Southwest
11. gummy
12. flowery
13. insider
14. a jogger
15. Mother's Day

3 Words That Mean the Same

1. perform
2. underneath
3. meadow
4. locate
5. upper
6. concept
7. message
8. jogger
9. total
10. chat

4 Word Opposites

1. hero
2. townspeople
3. straight
4. cause
5. disease
6. exhale
7. prompt
8. scaly
9. baggy
10. aware

Lesson 6

1 About the Reading

1. false
2. true
3. true
4. true
5. true
6. false
7. false
8. true
9. false

2 Working with Headings

Solids	Liquids	Gases
1. chestnut trees	1. blood	1. air
2. ice	2. orange juice	2. carbon dioxide
3. rocks	3. water	3. oxygen
4. steel	4. wine	4. steam

3 Compound Words

1. starfish
2. moonlighting
3. moonshine
4. skyscraper
5. skylight
6. cloudburst
7. skyline
8. sunstroke
9. sunflower
10. suntan

4 The Ending -*ing*

1. spelling	1. pleasing	1. beginning
2. crossing	2. mining	2. jogging
3. drawing	3. merging	3. rigging
4. coloring	4. boring	4. bidding
5. coating	5. daring	5. topping
6. belonging	6. carving	6. matting

5 Confusing -*ing* Words

1. staring, starring
2. baring, barring
3. gripping, griping
4. hoping, hopping
5. filling, filing

Lesson 7

1 About the Reading

1. Ohio
2. February 11, 1847
3. Michigan
4. three months
5. Al
6. He wanted to see if his friend would fly when he passed a lot of gas.
7. She was angry that his teacher thought he was crazy.
8. He had caused a fire in the baggage car.

9. He could concentrate without being interrupted by a lot of noise.
10. a. light bulb
    b. phonograph
    c. moving pictures
11. 84
12. He spent so much time working that he didn't have much time for a family.

2 Compound Words
1. hourglass
2. padlock
3. dishwasher
4. handcuffs
5. boxcar
6. screwdriver
7. jackhammer
8. sandpaper
9. pacemaker
10. gearshift
11. airplane
12. mousetrap

3 Which Word Fits Best?
1. disease
2. part
3. knapsack
4. liquid
5. ears
6. dinner
7. state
8. stare
9. result
10. stage

4 Syllables
1. re • ceive
2. sky • line
3. dish • wash • er
4. wor • ship
5. rail • way
6. be • gin • ning
7. deaf • ness
8. com • pound
9. jack • ham • mer

Lesson 8

1 About the Story
1. the spoon
2. Italy
3. People carried a knife with them that was used for everything, including cutting meat.
4. A knife goes to the right of the dinner plate.
5. a. soup
   b. to cut meat
   c. meat
   d. two
   e. one
   f. cutting the salad
6. how we came to use knives, forks, and spoons.
7. Answers may vary.

2 The Last Word on Knives
The Johnson boys' table manners are so crude that they probably would not be invited to a fancy dinner party.

3 Food for Thought
1. potatoes
2. boiling
3. stew
4. deep frying pan
5. pound
6. berries (possibly oranges)
7. Italy
8. teaspoon
9. breakfast or picnic
10. Thanksgiving

4 Singular and Plural Words
1. singular
2. plural
3. plural
4. singular
5. singular
6. singular
7. plural
8. plural
9. singular
10. plural
11. singular
12. singular

5 One Knife/Two Knives
knives
lives
shelves
leaves
loaves
halves

1. life
2. loaf
3. lives
4. loaves
5. knives
6. shelf
7. half
8. leaf
9. leaves
10. knife
11. shelves
12. halves

Lesson 9

1 About the Reading
1. Children would rather act the way they want to rather than the way adults want them to act.
2. Answers will vary.
3. Answers will vary.

2 Which Word Does Not Fit?
1. ice cream
2. manners
3. release
4. dinner
5. beet
6. pockets
7. food
8. billionth
9. automobile
10. pacemaker
11. Huron
12. feet

3 Recipes
Fried Chicken
1. Put flour, salt, pepper and chicken in paper bag.
2. Shake until chicken is well coated.
3. Melt butter or fat in deep frying pan.
4. Brown chicken slowly until skin is crisp and golden.
5. Drain on paper towels.

Green Salad
1. Wash greens and throw away any stems.
2. Tear into bite-size pieces.
3. Chill greens in bowl until serving time.
4. Just before serving, pour ¼ cup dressing over greens.
5. Toss lightly until dressing coats leaves.

4 Singular and Plural Words
1. bubble
2. channel
3. concept
4. desert
5. effect
6. league
7. meadow
8. menu
9. message
10. pocket

1. batteries
2. children
3. heroes
4. museums
5. spiders
6. strawberries
7. tongues
8. waitresses
9. women
10. Yankees

5 **More about Manners**

1. d   5. d   9. c
2. a   6. b   10. Answers will vary.
3. b   7. b
4. c   8. d

Lesson 10

1 **About the Reading**

1. France and the state of Washington
2. 1947
3. The man in Washington saw nine discs, whereas the Frenchman had seen only one.
4. a. weather balloons.
   b. small meteors
   c. large hailstones
5. A group connected with an Air Force base in Ohio studies flying saucers.
6. It is hard for some people to imagine things they have not experienced for themselves.
7. Answers will vary.
8. Answers will vary

2 **More about Meteors**

piece, space, hot, shine

because, stars

200,000,000 entering, explode, heard

collected, outside

3 **Choosing the Right Word**

1. disc   5. related   9. record
2. morning   6. Earth   10. sunglasses
3. stony   7. cloudburst
4. sun   8. concept

4 **Word Study**

1. racket   5. tears   9. lying
2. use   6. racket   10. wind
3. wind   7. use   11. lying
4. wound   8. wound   12. Tears

Review: Lessons 1-10

1 **Answer These Questions**

1. star   5. the light bulb
2. gases   6. deaf
3. disc   7. Italy
4. reach the Earth   8. Thanksgiving

2 **Word Study**

1. worship   6. fork
2. drawing   7. Italy
3. crudely   8. tongue
4. inventor   9. whirling
5. medicine   10. record

3 **Words That Mean the Same**

1. enter   7. sloppy
2. dining   8. sudden
3. continue   9. beam
4. connected   10. tale
5. release   11. swirl
6. pretend   12. entire

4 **Word Opposites**

1. worried   7. swallow
2. daring   8. immense
3. release   9. bottom
4. skyscraper   10. lying
5. believe in   11. downward
6. sloppy   12. narrow

5 **Syllables**

1. pocket   6. cavemen
2. waitress   7. cranberry
3. Michigan   8. strawberry
4. medicine   9. atmosphere
5. America   10. Huron

6 **Menus**

Breakfast	Thanksgiving Dinner	Picnic
1. corn flakes	1. apple pie	1. hamburgers
2. oatmeal	2. cranberry sauce	2. ketchup
3. orange juice	3. dressing	3. pickles
4. poached eggs	4. sweet potatoes	4. potato salad
5. toast	5. turkey	5. ants

7 **The Sound for _le_**

little, middle, able, gentle, apples, bubble, gobble, Bible

struggle

single, double

table

Lesson 11

1 **About the Reading**

1. a. false   f. false
   b. false   g. false
   c. true   h. false
   d. false   i. false
   e. true   j. false
2. Answers will vary.
3. Answers will vary.

2 **Changing the _y_ to _i_**

1. happier   happiest   happiness
2. lazier   laziest   laziness
3. lonelier   loneliest   loneliness
4. easier   easiest   easiness
5. moodier   moodiest   moodiness
6. busier   busiest   business

3 Word Endings

1. friendship	1. disagreement	1. deafness
2. worship	2. basement	2. loneliness
3. battleship	3. agreement	3. laziness
	4. statement	4. blindness
	5. apartment	5. happiness
		6. business

4 Silent Letters

1. gnat   6. fright
2. kneel   7. globe
3. wrench   8. sneeze
4. dumb   9. climb
5. fudge   10. misjudge

thumb
wrist
lamp
wren
numb
wrap

5 Happiness!

1. barber   6. February
2. Easter   7. happy
3. eighteen   8. moon
4. mammal   9. sign
5. knives   10. innings

Quote: Every human being is in some form seeking happiness.

Lesson 12

1 About the Author

1. Holland
2. twenty-five
3. Hitler
4. kill all Jews
5. Six million Jews were dead by the end of the war.
6. World War II
7. They needed to take many clothes with them, but they didn't dare carry a suitcase.
8. It was a small attic in Mr. Frank's office building.
9. a. They were loaded into cattle trucks.
   b. There was only one place to wash for 100 people.
   c. There were not enough bathrooms.
   d. Men, women, and children all slept together.
10. the English radio
11. Answers may vary. By giving her diary a name, it became sort of a friend she could talk to.
12. Answers will vary.

2 Word Beginnings

1. bookworm	7. Everywhere
2. committed	8. backfired
3. homeless	9. downfall
4. cattle	10. remind
5. misjudged	11. concept
6. unlikely	12. doormat

3 Words That Mean the Same

1. basement	6. perhaps
2. inmate	7. truly
3. M.D.	8. excite
4. inflate	9. dozen
5. slaughter	10. depressed

4 Word Opposites

1. disagreement	6. depressed
2. attic	7. accept
3. fever	8. blindness
4. outskirts	9. North Pole
5. cheap	10. glance

5 Words That End in Hard or Soft g

Soft g		Hard g	
badge	gorge	beg	jog
binge	misjudge	brag	shrug
garbage	verge	egg	underdog

Lesson 13

1 About the Reading

1. Anne seems to have the most trouble with her mother. Her mother apparently criticizes her with words and looks.
2. a. Peter wanted to see a movie.
   b. Peter's father and Anne's sister wanted a hot, leisurely bath.
   c. Peter's mother wanted to eat cream cakes.
   d. Anne's mother wanted a cup of coffee.
   e. Anne's father wanted to see a friend of his. (Also the dentist wanted to see his wife; Anne wanted a home of her own and the chance to return to school.)
3. She was not in Germany when the war broke out.
4. She believes that people are really good at heart.
5. Answers may vary.
6. Answers will vary.
7. Answers will vary.
8. Answers will vary.

2 World War II

money, changes, history

fifty, wounded, armed

invaded, countries, bombed, declared

3 Cities, States, and Countries

Cities	States	Countries
1. Amsterdam	1. California	1. Egypt
2. Baltimore	2. Hawaii	2. Germany
3. Boston	3. Michigan	3. Holland
4. Detroit	4. Ohio	4. Japan
5. Rome	5. Washington	5. Spain

4 Word Endings

1. picture, nature
2. attic, picnic
3. foolish, selfish
4. cattle, terrible
5. swallow, meadow
6. total, chemical
7. manager, message, baggage
8. wilderness, kindness, sadness

Lesson 14

1 About the Reading

1. the camel
2. Asia and Africa
3. fat
4. seventeen
5. a. Its lids and lashes protect its eyes.
   b. Its nostrils can close, protecting its nose from sand.
   c. Its strong teeth can chew nearly anything.
6. twenty-five miles
7. one thousand pounds
8. a. Camels can carry cargo across the desert.
   b. Its hair is used to make cloth, blankets, and tents.
   c. Its skin can be made into leather.
9. It has a bad temper.
10. Answers will vary.

2 Compound Words

1. duckpin
2. pigtail
3. beeline
4. foxhole
5. mousetrap
6. snakebite
7. piggyback
8. dogwood
9. fishbowl
10. birdhouse
11. sheepskin
12. monkeyshines

3 Word Endings

1. bracelet, blanket
2. produce, reduce
3. America, Africa
4. channel, camels
5. curdled, paddle
6. narrow, borrow
7. affected, rejected, collected
8. heaven's, dozen, chickens, kitchen

4 Syllables

1. car • gō
2. cur • dle
3. shăg • gy
4. kīnd • ness
5. cŏn • fūse
6. thŭn • der
7. frēe • ly
8. at • tăck
9. Ger • man
10. of • fice
11. ĭn • māte
12. per • hăps
13. ŭn • păck
14. Hŏl • land
15. Ăm • ster • dăm
16. ō • ver • hang • ing

Lesson 15

1 About the Reading

1. a. southpaw   e. twenty million
   b. Italy   f. right-handed
   c. 1903   g. left
   d. hooker   h. oxygen

2. a. false   f. false
   b. true   g. false
   c. true   h. true
   d. true   i. false
   e. true   j. true

2 "Handy" Sayings

1. c
2. a
3. b
4. a
5. d
6. b
7. c
8. d

3 "Handy" Words

1. handlebar
2. handball
3. handshake
4. handbag
5. handful
6. handcuff
7. handsome
8. handle
9. handy
10. handpick

4 Singular and Plural Words

Singular	Plural
1. leaf	leaves
2. half	halves
3. employer	employers
4. ox	oxen
5. lash	lashes
6. deer	deer
7. diary	diaries
8. bicycle	bicycles
9. unit	units
10. cow	cattle

Review: Lessons 1-15

1 Answer These Questions

1. Adolf Hitler
2. 1945
3. Japan or Italy
4. Anne Frank
5. Holland
6. camel
7. Asia and Africa
8. fat
9. southpaws
10. twenty million

2 Word Study

1. throw it slowly
2. piggies
3. the United States
4. past
5. Yellow
6. breathing
7. start a fire
8. wet
9. solid
10. culture

3 Matching
1. Mr.   5. etc.
2. IOU   6. A.M.
3. Ms.   7. Dr.
4. Mrs.   8. B.C.

4 Matching
1. English   3. German   5. Dutch
2. French   4. Greek   6. American

5 Meet Ms. Brown
1. kindhearted   5. handicapped
2. lazy   6. moody, accepting
3. selfish   7. clumsy
4. foolish   8. confused, loneliness

6 Spelling Check
1. Holland   5. radio
2. Texas   6. dentist
3. truly   7. student
4. wages   8. Germany

7 Syllables
1. hand • cuff   9. fish • bowl
2. pro • tect   10. duck • pin
3. pig • tail   11. lone • li • ness
4. state • ment   12. un • com • mon
5. there • fore   13. wil • der • ness
6. de • press   14. mis • fit
7. bee • line   15. a • gree • ment
8. it • self   16. dis • a • gree • ment

Lesson 16
1 About the Reading
1. a   3. b   5. c   7. b   9. d
2. a   4. c   6. c   8. b   10. b

2 About the Reading
1. A living thing is badly hurt.
2. Hormones are released.
3. There is no pain
4. The living thing becomes calm.
5. Death happens without a struggle.

3 The Ending -ly
differently   awfully
narrowly   nervously
suddenly   entirely
foolishly   strictly
mostly   promptly

1. narrowly   6. strictly
2. promptly   7. suddenly
3. entirely   8. mostly
4. nervously   9. awfully
5. foolishly   10. differently

4 The Ending -ly
1. easily   5. unluckily
2. bodily   6. speedily
3. busily   7. happily
4. greedily   8. clumsily

5 Compound Words
1. deadline   6. sunset
2. newsstand   7. neighborhood
3. overheard   8. lowdown
4. campground   9. jackhammers
5. freeway   10. outhouses

Lesson 17
1 About the Reading
1. 1856 to 1917
2. as a salesman
3. He collected diamond jewelry.
4. He planned to eat all the desserts on the platter.
5. His stomach rubbed against the table.
6. The doctors advised him to eat properly.
7. He thought that eating reasonable amounts of food would take all the fun out of eating.
8. He died in an Atlantic City hotel of overeating.
9. Answers will vary.

2 Food for Thought
1. Apple   6. dough (bread)
2. lemon   7. beef
3. chicken   8. honey
4. toast   9. crab
5. bread (dough) 10. Cheese

3 The Ending -ful
bagful   shameful
colorful   spiteful
delightful   successful
faithful   tearful
graceful   wishful
respectful   wonderful

1. colorful   7. tearful
2. Faithful   8. respectful
3. successful   9. shameful
4. wishful   10. delightful
5. spiteful   11. graceful
6. bagful   12. wonderful

4 Working with Syllables
1. vegetables   6. vanilla, chocolate, strawberry
2. oyster   7. restaurant
3. yogurt   8. spaghetti
4. doughnuts   9. menu
5. salad   10. breakfast

Lesson 18

1 About the Reading

1. false	6. false
2. true	7. true
3. true	8. true
4. false	9. false
5. false	10. false

2 More about Potatoes

writer

mountains, wheat, pieces, instead, bread

explored, Spain

brought, 1621, Ireland, settled

3 Where Would You Find It?

1. vines	8. purse
2. fork	9. piano
3. Italy	10. Holland
4. restaurant	11. ocean
5. bottle	12. stadium
6. jail	13. street
7. hotel	14. New England

4 The Ending -less

hitless	priceless
faultless	speechless
sugarless	strapless
pointless	treeless

1. sugarless	5. hitless
2. priceless	6. speechless
3. Strapless	7. faultless
4. treeless	8. pointless

Lesson 19

1 About the Reading

1. pints	6. large intestine.
2. small intestine.	7. What the person likes to eat
3. relaxed.	8. solid to liquid
4. waste.	9. glands.
5. makes food soft.	10. how food is digested.

2 More about Digestion

1. Teeth — break up food into small bits
2. Stomach — turns the food into a semi-liquid mass
3. Small intestine — digests the food
4. Large intestine — stores waste from food

3 Cause and Effect

1. The stomach has to work harder at churning the food.
2. It passes into the large intestine.
3. The person feels tired and upset.
4. The body can become diseased.

4 The Human Body

1. stomach	6. large intestine
2. glands	7. heart
3. lungs	8. muscles
4. liver	9. pancreas
5. small intestine	10. spleen

5 Word Endings

1. mentioned, digestion
2. Moments, agreement
3. continued, blue, tissues
4. settled, bottle, apple
5. pocket, blanket, racket
6. America, soda, saliva
7. handle, paddle, muscles
8. managed, message, cabbage
9. certain, curtains, mountain
10. ideal, hospital, chemicals

Lesson 20

1 About the Story

1. She was angry at him.
2. She was happy with him.
3. The young man has won her over with his charm and his soup.
4. He gives her the nail and tells her not to use it until she has nothing else to eat.
5. Answers may vary.
6. Nail soup, in this story, is a vegetable soup. The nail served only as a catalyst to obtain the other ingredients.
7. The young man is not a beggar. Granny willingly offered him the ingredients he needed for the soup.

2 May I Take Your Order?

1. a. $2.50
   b. $5.05
   c. $1.80
2. Iced tea is not available. (It's out of season.)
3. Probably you would try to talk a young child into ordering "Kid Stuff."
4. Answers will vary.
5. Answers will vary.

3 Same or Opposite?

1. same	9. opposite
2. same	10. same
3. same	11. opposite
4. opposite	12. opposite
5. same	13. opposite
6. same	14. same
7. opposite	15. same
8. opposite	